A Float of Crocodiles /
Una manada de cocodrilos

By Karlie Gambino

Traducción al español: Eduardo Alamán

Gareth Stevens
Publishing

Please visit our website, www.garethstevens.com. For a free color catalog of all our high-quality books, call toll free 1-800-542-2595 or fax 1-877-542-2596.

Library of Congress Cataloging-in-Publication Data

First Edition

Published in 2013 by
Gareth Stevens Publishing
111 East 14th Street, Suite 349
New York, NY 10003

Designer: Ben Gardner
Editor: Greg Roza

Photo credits: Cover, p. 1 © iStockphoto.com/Alan Smithers; interior backgrounds Daniiel/Shutterstock.com; p. 5 Jason Edwards/National Geographic/Getty Images; p. 7 Uryadnikov Sergey/Shutterstock.com; p. 9 Vladimir Koletic/Shutterstock.com; p. 11 © iStockphoto.com/Сергей Урядников; p. 13 © iStockphoto.com/sombutt kaewjunchai; p. 15 kavram/Shutterstock.com; p. 17 Sergey Starostin/Shutterstock.com; p. 19 Martin Harvey/Peter Arnold/Getty Images; p. 20 saiko3p/Shutterstock.com; p. 21 Debora Atuy/Flickr/Getty Images.

Printed in the United States of America

CPSIA compliance information: Batch #CW13GS: For further information contact Gareth Stevens, New York, New York at 1-800-542-2595.

Contents

- -

Contenido

Floating with Crocodiles

Crocodiles, or crocs, are **reptiles**. They live in rivers, lakes, and **swamps** in warm places around the world. A group of crocs is called a float when it's in the water. It's called a bask when the crocs are on land.

- -

Flotando con cocodrilos

Los cocodrilos son **reptiles**. Viven en ríos, lagos o **pantanos** en climas cálidos por todo el mundo. Un grupo de cocodrilos se llama manada. A los cocodrilos les gusta tumbarse al sol.

5

Happy Together

Crocodiles like to be with other crocodiles. A float may have mothers, fathers, and young crocs. It may include other crocs, too. In large floats, crocs can often be seen resting next to and even on top of each other.

Juntos y felices

A los cocodrilos les gusta estar juntos. Una manada puede tener mamás, papás y cocodrilos jóvenes. Además puede tener otros cocodrilos. En manadas grandes es común que los cocodrilos descansen juntos y hasta se tumben unos sobre otros.

A Lot of Crocs!

The number of crocodiles in a float depends on how much food is around. The more food there is, the bigger the float. A float can have as few as two crocodiles or as many as 100.

- -

¡Muchos cocodrilos!

El número de cocodrilos en una manada depende de la comida disponible. Si hay mucha comida la manada es más grande. Una manada puede tener solo dos cocodrilos o puede tener más de 100.

Meat Eaters

Crocodiles eat meat. They hide in water and wait for animals to come near. Quickly, they jump forward and grab the animals with their strong **jaws**. The crocs in a float may work together to catch and eat dinner!

Carnívoros

Los cocodrilos comen carne. Los cocodrilos se esconden en el agua y esperan a que se acerque un animal. Rápidamente, el cocodrilo salta y atrapa al animal con sus fuertes **mandíbulas**. ¡Los cocodrilos pueden trabajar en equipo para conseguir su cena!

Digging In

Crocodiles live where it gets very hot. They stay cool by lying in water. When the weather is cooler, they dig **burrows** to lay in. The crocs in a float sometimes work together to dig large burrows.

- -

Excavando

Los cocodrilos viven en lugares muy calientes. Se refrescan cuando están en el agua. Cuando el clima es más frío, los cocodrilos cavan **guaridas** para recostarse. En ocasiones, los cocodrilos de una manada trabajan juntos para cavar guaridas grandes.

13

Who's in Charge?

The largest and oldest crocs in a float are in charge. They get to eat first while the others wait their turn. The largest crocs also get the best places to sun themselves and the best burrows.

¿Quién es el jefe?

Los cocodrilos más grandes y viejos son los jefes de la manada. Estos cocodrilos comen primero y los demás deben esperar su turno. Además, los cocodrilos más grandes eligen los mejores lugares para tumbarse bajo el sol y para descansar en las guaridas.

15

Croc Talk

The crocodiles in a float **communicate** with each other. They move in special ways, and they touch each other. They also use lots of sounds to communicate. Crocs hiss, grunt, cough, growl, and roar!

- -

Lenguaje de cocodrilos

Los cocodrilos de una manada **se comunican** entre sí. Para esto se mueven o se tocan de manera especial. Además hacen muchos ruidos para comunicarse. ¡Los cocodrilos silban, gruñen, tosen y rugen!

17

Baby Crocs

Mother crocodiles lay eggs on land. The babies squeak just before breaking out of their eggs. The mother takes care of her babies. She carries them to water in her mouth. Fathers may help care for young crocs, too.

Cocodrilos bebé

Las mamás cocodrilo ponen huevos en la tierra. Los bebés chillan antes de salir del huevo. La mamá cuida a los bebés. La mamá los lleva al agua en su hocico. Los papás también cuidan a los bebés cocodrilo.

19

Crocs of the World

Did you know there are 14 kinds of crocodiles in the world? The smallest are dwarf crocodiles. The biggest are saltwater crocodiles. They can grow to be 20 feet (6 m) long!

Cocodrilos en el mundo

Hay más de 14 tipos de cocodrilos en el mundo. Los más pequeños son los enanos. Los más grandes son los cocodrilos de agua salada. ¡Pueden tener hasta 20 pies (6 m) de largo!

Fun Facts About Crocodiles/
Datos curiosos sobre los cocodrilos

Crocodiles have been on Earth since the time of the dinosaurs.

Los cocodrilos habitan el planeta desde el tiempo de los dinosaurios.

Crocs can live up to 70 years in the wild.

Los cococrilos pueden vivir hasta 70 años.

Mother crocodiles can lay up to 90 eggs at one time.

Las mamás cocodrilo pueden poner hasta 90 huevos.

Crocodiles are great swimmers, but they can also run on land.

Los cocodrilos son muy buenos nadadores. También pueden correr.

Glossary

burrow: a hole made by an animal in which it hides or lives

communicate: to share ideas and feelings through sounds and motions

jaw: the bones that hold the teeth and make up the mouth

reptile: an animal that has scales, breathes air, and lays eggs. Turtles, snakes, crocodiles, and lizards are reptiles.

swamp: an area with trees that is covered with water at least part of the time

- -

Glosario

comunicarse: compartir ideas por medio de sonidos y movimientos

guarida (la): un hoyo donde vive o se esconde un animal

mandíbula (la): los huesos que alojan los dientes y forman la boca

pantano (el): un area con árboles que esta cubierta con agua parte del tiempo.

reptil (el): un animal con escamas que respira oxígeno y pone huevos. Las tortugas y las serpientes también son reptiles.

For More Information/ Para más información

Books

Antill, Sara. *A Crocodile's Life*. New York, NY: PowerKids Press, 2012.

Sexton, Colleen. *The Saltwater Crocodile*. Minneapolis, MN: Bellwether Media, 2012.

Websites

The Crocodile Hunter
www.crocodilehunter.com.au
Learn more about crocodiles and other wild animals on this fun website.

Nile Crocodiles
kids.nationalgeographic.com/kids/animals/creaturefeature/nile-crocodile
Read about the Nile crocodile, see pictures, and watch a video of a mother with her babies.

Index

Índice